# The Pizza, the Peach & the
# PLATYPUS

## Creating *Your* Life of Wonder

## Mike Robertson

MIKEY'S IMAGINATION PUBLISHING

Austin

A Division of Shadownoze, Inc.,
A completely imaginary company
www.IsThisMikeOn.com

ISBN: 147757266X
EAN-13:9781477572665

First printing • September 2014

Mike Robertson
1507 Newfield Lane
Austin, TX  78703

Visit www.IsThisMikeOn.com for updates and additional info.

Published by Mikey's Imagination

This book is dedicated to:

Brian Wilson

Julius Henry Marx

Winsor McCay

*"Every child is an artist, the problem is staying an artist when you grow up"*
— Pablo Picasso

*"Creativity is just connecting things. When you ask creative people how they did something, they feel a little guilty because they didn't really do it, they just saw something. It seemed obvious to them after a while"*
— Steve Jobs

*"We don't look backwards for very long. We keep moving forward, opening up new doors and doing new things, because we're curious...and curiosity keeps leading us down new paths."*
— Walt Disney

Mike Robertson

# 1.

# RIGHT HERE IN BLACK & WHITE

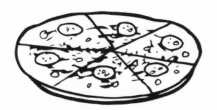

Mike Robertson

Life is art.

I don't mean that *living* is an art, I mean that life is art just like painting is art or composing music is art or sculpting or playing the violin or writing a book.

Let's use the book analogy.

Every day, you add a page to your book, the book of your life. It's not written in ink or in pixels on a screen; it's written in the annals of time, in the history of life on earth. It is a record of one human being's actions, dreams, laughter, and tears.

You wake up each morning to a blank page and by the time you go to bed that evening, you're going to fill that page with something.

But what?

Would you buy a book in which every page contained the same words as the page before? No, of course not; that would be one boring, tedious book.

So why write your life that way? Why do the same things over and over, waiting for something to change, waiting for excitement or circumstance or luck to show up and make the next page something more interesting?

Listen. Here's the whole thing right here:

You are the author.

YOU.

You hold the pencil in your hand and the blank page sits before you. And you write pretty much the same thing you did yesterday.

And you wonder why your story didn't turn out to be as interesting as you hoped.

There's a better way to live.

It's the most beloved movie of all time, the 1939 film called *The Wonderful Wizard of Oz*. You're probably familiar with the story, how a young girl named Dorothy is growing up in a bleak place, a flat, dusty, sepia-toned world called Kansas. Apparently an orphan, Dorothy is being raised by her Aunt Em and Uncle Henry on a ramshackle farm, far from town or neighbors…or fun or excitement. Besides her aunt and uncle, Dorothy's only human companions are the three less-than-spectacular farmhands: Hunk, Hickory, and Zeke. Her closest friend, though, is her small dog, Toto.

Dorothy's world is not one of enchantment. The landscape is barren. Auntie Em and Uncle Henry are always busy, as are the farm-hands. And Toto has made an enemy in the local spinster with the euphonious name of Almira Gulch. Toto's habit of digging in Miss Gulch's garden has culminated with him nipping the old sourpuss on the leg. And now Miss Gulch has permission from the sherif to confis-cate the dog and have him destroyed.

Poor Dorothy. Her life is stuck in a black-and-white rut. Told by her aunt to find a place where she won't get into any trouble, Dorothy wonders if there really is such a place…perhaps over the rainbow?

Toto escapes from Miss Gulch and returns to Dorothy, but she knows it won't be long before he'll be taken again. She decides to run away. But her journey is cut short by a phony fortune teller who convinces her to go back home—in a hurry—because there's a storm coming.

Back at the farm, everyone looks for Dorothy, but they have to head into the storm cellar because an incredible tornado is coming. When Dorothy gets home, she can't find anyone and is unable to get into the cellar, so she seeks shelter from the storm inside the farmhouse. The tornado blows furiously, sending the window frame careening into the room and knocking the young girl unconscious. Her home is whooshed up into the tornado, spinning like a toP, until it comes to rest with a thud.

Tentatively, Dorothy makes her way to the front door of the little house, slowly opening it.

And she is in another world. It's a world of bright colors and gigantic plants and ruby slippers and talking trees and wicked witches.

When Dorothy opens the door, the vision of Munchkinland is awe-inspiring. Her black-and-white world is gone, replaced by a Technicolor wonderland.

Is that how you remember it?

My experience was a bit different.

I came of age in a time before streaming video and Netflix, a time before DVDs, even before VHS and Blockbuster ruled the world. When I was a kid, I had one chance per year to see *The Wizard of Oz*. CBS would show the movie, usually around the Thanksgiving-Christmas holidays, and families would gather to watch, an occurrence that became a tradition.

Each year, I sprawled on the living room floor, watching as Dorothy opened the door of her farmhouse and stepped into awe. I was awe-struck, too.

There's just one thing.

We had a black-and-white television set.

When Dorothy opened that door, I saw the giant flowers and the Good Witch's bubble and the Lullaby League and the Lollipop Guild…and I thought it was magnificent.

I didn't know there was *more*.

That, I believe, is one of the most important thoughts I've ever had. Most people go through life, experiencing the ups and downs, and they think, "This is okay. It's a good life. I'm pretty lucky."

It never enters their mind that perhaps they're only seeing the black-and-white version. It's true, you can enjoy life and have wonderful experiences and still miss out on this all-important fact:

There's Technicolor out there.

I thought *The Wizard of Oz* was great, fine, perfect…but I had never seen the full spectrum. Once I did, I began to wonder what *else* I was missing out on.

That's the big question: if your whole life up to now was just black and white, what might the Technicolor version be like?

I can tell you.

It's amazing, hilarious, enchanting and thrilling.

And you can see it for yourself.

This is a book about creativity. It's not a scholarly book; I don't have any acronyms after my name, nothing special in the way of education. But I do know how to be creative and I emphatically know that—by thinking creatively—life can suddenly bloom with color and interest and refreshing possibilities.

I'm not going to talk about the technical aspects of the brain or cite scientific research on creativity.

I'm gonna tell you stories. Stories that repeatedly proved to me the benefits of approaching life from a creative mindset. Stories are how we learn and they're what we tend to remember most. You're writing one right now. Is it an interesting story or a snooze? You're the author, remember? You can decide to make something fantastic happen on the very next page.

And you should.

In one of Rosalind Russell's best films, *Auntie Mame*, her irrepressible character makes a proclamation that we should all embroider on a pillow and look at daily: "Life is a banquet and most poor suckers are starving to death."

Or, to paraphrase: "Life is art…and most poor suckers never even sharpen their pencil."

There's more. Let's go find it.

2.

# THE BLANK CANVAS

On the day you are born, you're given a canvas, pristine and white and empty. One of the most important decisions you will ever make is how you're going to fill that space. Far too many folks get to the end of life and say, "Here's my canvas, still as pretty and white as the day I got it…still got the shrink-wrap on it, in fact."

That, my friends, is a tragedy.

Life is not supposed to be a spectator sport. Life is about making your mark, scribbling at least the equivalent of "Kilroy Was Here." A blank canvas is a life without experiment, risk or adventure.

Without art.

Other people take a different approach. They find someone successful or talented or famous and they say, "I'm going to do exactly what that person did," and they try to follow every step their role model took. The result is something that looks like a bad photocopy of someone else's painting.

I went to the Louvre earlier this year. I knew there was no way I could see even one percent of the masterpieces on display there. But I was determined I would make a beeline for the Mona Lisa, the most famous painting in history. It's not hard to find; just follow the mob.

My wife and I wormed and weaseled our way to the front of the Mona mosh pit, taking our selfies and gazing for a fEw seconds on that enigmatic painting, surrounded by hundreds of people trying to do the same. Think about that for a moment: people, mobbing…for art.

If the Louvre announced that they were going to exhibit a photo-copy of the Mona Lisa in a different part of the museum, how many people would go see it? How long a line would you stand in to look at a Xerox of the Mona Lisa?

The idea is ludicrous. The painting is priceless because it's one of a kind; it's unique. It would be pointless to make a copy of it.

So why are you trying to copy someone else's life? We don't need another flawed copy of Mona Lisa.

We need *your* painting, even if—no, *especially* if—it's different from anything ever painted before.

Noted speaker and author Jim Rohn put it like this: "If you don't design your own life plan, chances are you'll fall into someone else's plan. And guess what they have planned for you? Not much."

That's why you need to learn to think creatively. When you quit trying to follow someone else's footsteps and forge your own path, you are going to find life becomes much more exciting and your own story/painting/symphony becomes a unique masterpiece.

I've found that—once you get off the beaten path—there's very little traffic out on the road less traveled. And what a trip you're in for!

Think more creatively. That's what I'm saying.

Oh, and I can hear what many of you are saying back to me: "I'm not a very creative person."

Poppycock.

Balderdash.

Fiddlesticks.

You *are* creative. What did you do when you woke up this morning? Did you study your script for the day? Did you look over the lines you would be saying to each person you bumped into?

Nope. You made it up as you went along. You improvised like a jazz musician; you just didn't do it on the saxophone. You wailed, baby!

Here's a piece of music that an orchestra member might play:

Every note is written down. There are instructions for when to play loudly and when to play softly. You don't really have to make any choices; everything is literally laid out in black and white.

Contrast that with what a jazz player might see on his music stand at the point he is supposed to play a solo:

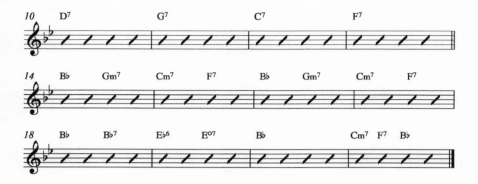

Not a single note is written down. Five seconds before he starts playing his solo, he doesn't know what's going to happen. All his lessons, every song he's ever played or even heard, how he's feeling, how the drummer is playing…all these things and more will combine to allow him to launch off into uncharted territory, to play something that has never been played before and likely will never be played again in the exact same way.

Life should be jazz. Always riffing, always experimenting, always channeling the past to proclaim the present and hope for the future.

Do you want to play the notes that somebody else came up with? Or do you want to make your own song?

# 3.

# THE FORMULA

Three little words.

No, not "I love you," although that little trio can be life-changing.

I've got three words to help you open that creaky, cobwebbed door to your creative mind, the part of your brain that may have been dormant for a long, long time.

When we're children, we are all creative. We paint and draw a lot. We make up our own songs while we're on the swing set. We tell incredible lies to get out of trouble. We have imaginary friends and monsters under the bed and secret hideouts and nobody even knows that we are really superheroes.

What happened to that kid you used to be?

School.

Grades.

Parents.

Job.

Performance reviews.

Responsibility.

Life.

Somewhere inside you, that kid is waiting for you to unlock the cell you slammed shut years ago. He wants to come out and play. He wants to have amazing adventures again. He wants to go to Oz and live where there's Technicolor.

And three words can help you awaken the child, the creativity, the fun. It's not something you have to go acquire; it's already there, dormant.

The words are short, easy to remember. I even made them rhyme so you can never forget.

SKILL

DRILL

THRILL

These three may not sound much like "Abra-cadabra" or "Presto Change-o," but they're just as magical. Let's dig a little deeper into each one.

Skill.

What can you do well? What's a talent or ability you have that is not shared by everyone else? Please notice I did not ask what do you *wish* you could do? The SKILL involved in this formula is something you already have. It's hard-wired into your being. It comes naturally to you.

And because of that, perhaps you undervalue it. It's all too easy to look at other people's skills and pooch out your pouty lower lip and say, "*That's* the skill I want!"

It's not yours. Their skill, their talent seems so wonderful to us and we tell ourselves that if we only work hard enough or do sufficient study or pay enough money thAt we could do what they do.

That way lies heartbreak, my friend. It's trying to paint someone else's Mona Lisa instead of figuring out your own.

So I ask again, what can you do? Put some thought into this. You might be looking in all the wrong places. I've known so many people who say, "I have no talent. I can't sing, can't play an instrument, can't draw a straight line, can't write, can't dance…I can't do anything!" Look in some other areas, then. Can you cook? Can you listen? Can you walk far? Can you make someone laugh? Can you ask people for money? Can you see problems earlier than others?

There's something you're already good at. If you can't come up with an answer on your own, ask someone who knows you well. "What can I do really well?" I'll bet they can see the answer right away.

When they tell you what you do well, you may think, "That's not very valuable." Cut it out. Stop thinking that way. We're going to find a way to make it valuable.

The SKILL is the thing (or perhaps more than one thing) that you can do well. It's your gift, even if it doesn't seem special to you right now.

The second word is DRILL.

Every soldier understands the meaning of that word. To drill is to repeat something over and over, practicing it, honing it, making it better and better.

That SKILL, which doesn't seem very special to you at the moment, will get more valuable when you do the drill.

Have you ever been at home during a thunderstorm, listening to the rain and wind, seeing the occasional flashes of lightning…and then the lights go out? You feel your way into the kitchen and dig through the drawer or cabinet until you find the flashlight and you flip the switch.

And the batteries are dead.

You didn't do the drill. You gotta check the batteries. You gotta put oil in the car engine. You gotta keep your sword sharpened. Because when the enemy attacks, there's no time to say, "I can handle this, but first I need to go take a course in self-defense."

The drill is what will make your skill into something wonderfully useful. But if you don't do the drill, your talent may get rusty and weak; it may even dwindle away to nothing.

The third word is THRILL.

Having a skill and doing the drill to make it the best it can possibly be is fine, but it takes a thrilling idea to get you into Technicolor territory. It's the most challenging of the three words. Thrilling ideas are not always easy to conjure. They do, however, come easier when you practice looking for them.

That's the formula. SKILL/DRILL/THRILL. It sounds too simple, right? But I'm going to share with you some stories of how that simple formula changed my life—and the lives of some other people—in dramatic and incredible ways.

# 4.

# WHEN THE CHIPS ARE DOWN

Most of the stories I'm going to share are my own. But I have grown to recognize that many people have used the three-word formula—even without identifying them—to find their own paths.

People like Debbi.

Debbi grew up in Oakland, California, one of five children in a family that had to stretch every penny. They didn't even have a washing machine. Debbi was only 19 when she married a young college graduate named Randy, and she found herself a housewife like her own mother had been. Randy was hoping to start an investment firm and he and Debbi were invited to dinner at the home of a potential client. Debbi was impressed with the massive iron gates and the huge house.

She found herself sitting in the library of the posh residence and the owner asked her a simple question. "Debbi, what do you want to do with your life?"

Debbi, unable to come up with a master plan but wishing to

appear somewhat sophisticated in front of this man, said, "Well, I'm just trying to get orientated."

The man pulled a large dictionary off the shelf and dropped it in her lap, saying, "The word is *oriented*, not orientated. If you can't speak the English language, you shouldn't speak at all."

Embarrassed and ashamed, Debbi burst into tears as the man left the room. But she made an important decision. She vowed that she would never let anyone make her feel that way again. She wanted to be a somebody, instead of a nobody.

But how? What was her SKILL? She could only think of one thing. She liked to bake cookies, had been doing it since before she was a teenager. That's all she had.

Pay attention to this: Debbi didn't decide to go back to college or take a continuing eduCation course or take lessons in doing something "more valuable." She recognized her skill and chose that skill to be her ticket to better things.

So she did the drill. She recognized that she had to use the best ingredients, even if they were more expensive. She baked tray after tray of cookies, testing them on friends and family. She had no money and no prior business experience. She went from bank to bank, trying to get a loan to open her THRILLing idea: a cookie store.

At each bank, the officers would eat the cookies, tell Debbi how wonderful they were, and then turn her down for a loan. After many attempts, she was finally able to get a loan with a whopping 21% interest rate. Even her own husband bet her that she wouldn't be able to make fifty dollars on her first day of business.

But Debbi Fields was determined to be somebody. She went up

and down the street near her shop, giving out free samples, and managed to sell $75 worth of cookies that day.

Today, Mrs. Fields Cookies is a $300 million business. Debbi Fields is a beautiful example of someone identifying her skill, following a drill to perfect her product, and having the thrilling idea of opening a cookie store, a considerably more novel idea in 1977 than it would be today.

Skill/Drill/Thrill is a powerful formula. It changed Debbi Fields' life dramatically.

Now I want to tell you how it changed mine.

# 5.

# THE QUESTION, POPPED

In 1986, I was a single guy who had never been married. I was 32, and beginning to consider the idea that I might never get married at all. I wasn't against the idea; my parents were married for 60 years, so I had a great example to follow. And it's not that I was unsuitable "marriage material." I didn't have trouble finding a date. I just hadn't found "the one."

That's when I met Lisa. She was a lovely, talented woman who also had not found anyone she considered marrying. We started to date and we got along well. Over the next few months, my feelings for her continued to grow and I eventually was convinced that the moment had finally arrived and Lisa was indeed THE ONE.

I began to think about proposing. But I had been a creative person my entire life and I did not want to pop the question in some way that had been done by millions of other people.

I considered many options. Perhaps an ad in the newspaper? Nah, I knew that had been done lots of time, plus it didn't seem all that "special" to me.

How about renting a billboard? I liked the thought of it, but once again I had read stories of other people who had done it that way.

I had to focus. What would be the best way for me to pop the question? Was there some skill or talent I could use to accomplish this most-meaningful task?

Hmmm. There *was* one thing. I had always loved music and I was singing from the time I could make a sound. When I was 13, I'd taught myself to play the guitar so that I could accompany myself when I sang. I started writing songs...bad songs. When I know you better, perhaps I'll sing *Tryin' To Convince Myself*, the first song I ever wrote. But I'll probably never know you well enough to risk that. You're welcome.

A couple of years later, I switched to the piano and found it suited me better than the guitar. I went to college as a music major, where I had to sing in German and French and Latin. That was wasted on me, because I wanted to be Billy Joel or Elton John. As it turned out, there was already one of each. Even so, I was pretty good at playing and singing. I had a real skill.

I supposed I could have just sung Lisa a song while sitting at a piano or while I played the guitar, but there had to be a better solution.

Although I didn't realize it at the time, I had already done a great deal of drill work to sharpen my skill. Not only had I learned to play several instruments, and put in countless hours of practicing, I had studied songwriting. I'd read books on composition, and pored over interviews with songwriters. I would study hit songs and see wHy this chord was better than that chord. I learned that it was simple to write a moon/June/soon type of lyric and I could recognize when I was lapsing into cliché.

So I decided to write a proposal song, one that clearly asked Lisa to marry me.

Meh.

That was a decent idea, but it felt like there was still something missing. I had the skill and had done the drill, but the idea of just singing my song to her did not have the thrill I was seeking. I needed to up the ante, to step up my game.

I grew up glued to the radio. I vividly remember on the last day of 1968 as I sprawled on the floor, copying down the top 100 songs of the year as KTSA played them in reverse order. I even remember how ridiculous it was that the Beatles' *Hey Jude* came in at number two, while the top spot for the year was *Love Is Blue* by—uh—Paul Mauriat.

Radio was how I heard the music that was the soundtrack of my life. What could be more exciting than having a song on the radio? What if I could get a radio station to play my song and Lisa heard me—on the airwaves—asking her to marry me?

Hello, thrilling idea. Now I just had to make it happen.

First, I wrote the song. Then I revised the song. Then I changed some words. Over a two-week period, I polished the song until it felt right. I liked the melody, the chords, the lyrics; it didn't feel like a copy of any other song.

Of course, I would have to record the song for it to be on the radio, since my plan was to be sitting next to Lisa when the song played. And I didn't have any money to hire musicians or invest in endless hours in a recording studio. I did own a synthesizer, a very primitive drum machine, and a unit that could record four tracks on a regular cassette tape. I did a demo version of the song, laying down a drum track, a bass part, three keyboard parts, and my vocal. I was able to do all those parts, because I had done the drill work. Finally satisfied that the song would work, I still wanted a higher quality recording that could only be done in a real studio.

I priced several studios in Austin and found one where I could actually afford a couple of hours of recording time. I hauled my synth into the studio and recorded one track at a time, rarely doing more than one take because my time was so limited. When the tracks were done, I coached the engineer through the mixing part and finished just as my time—and budget—came to an end.

I left the studio with a cassette of my song. The title? *The Question, Popped.* Get it? I was making "pop" music out of the big "question."

Now it was time for the hard part. I had told my family about my big plan. They were skeptical, and with good reason. Getting a song on the radio is not easy. But I had to try.

I went to visit the station I usually listened to, and spoke to a deejay there, told him my grand, romantic dream and how he could help make it come true. He looked at me with a piteous smirk and said, "Can't play anything that's not on the playlist, my man."

On to the next, a "morning zoo" style station that was highly rated in Austin. I again recited my thrilling idea to a deejay and two of his sidekicks. When I was done, he looked at the other two and said, "I dunno. We certainly couldn't play the whole thing. We might be able to play part of it…We'd have to have some fun with it, of course."

"What do you mean?"

"Well, we would have to poke some fun, ya know? I mean, we wouldn't throw *up* on it or anything, but…"

He wanted to make a joke out of the most important moment in my life? No, thanks.

When my mother heard this part of the story, she gently said, "Honey, no radio station is going to play a song by someone they've never heard of."

If I had given up at that point, I would have proven her right.

But I had a thrilling idea! It was a *good* idea. It needed to happen.

I called station number three. I really didn't listen to this station much, because they were the heavy metal station. But I was running out of options. The program director agreed to meet with me, so I went to his office and told him my big, silly, romantic idea. He rocked back and forth in his chair, considering it.

"Let me hear the song," he said. It was a smart move on his part; I could have been absolutely terrible at singing, playing and writing. He did not want to commit to something that might come back to bite him in the ASCAP. (If you get that joke, bless your heart!)

He popped my cassette into a stereo unit behind him and hit the "play" button. He listened to about 20 seconds of the song and said, "Okay, yeah, we'll do it."

Yes!

"When do you wanna do it?" asked this wonderful, caring, obviously discerning and intelligent gentleman.

I had a plan. I was going to propose on the anniversary of my first

date with Lisa. We had decided to celebrate our twelve-month relation-
ship by spending the day together, shopping, eating, taking pictures,
maybe seeing a movie.

Picking the day was easy. Choosing the location was a bit more
involved. I decided to do it at the Zilker Botanical Garden in Austin.
Not only was it a beautiful, peaceful place, it was also the place where
Lisa's father had proposed to her mother. Isn't it great when a plan
comes together?

I arranged with the radio program director for the song to be
played about 3:15 on the appointed day. I would have a jam box with
me in the garden so that we could hear the song. Let's see, what else
could I throw into the mix?

This was before video cameras were as ubiquitous as they would
soon become. I certainly didn't have one, so I wouldn't be able to
videotape the proposal. What I did have, however, was something
very cool. I had bought a Stereo Realist camera, made in the 1950s,
when 3D photography was the next big thing. The Realist used regular
35mm film, but it had two lenses on the front, spaced the same dis-
tance apart as your eyeballs. When the shutter was clicked, the camera
took two photos, from slightly different angles. Once the two images
were mounted in a slide frame, a special viewer would allow you to see
the photo in a very good quality three-dimensional simulation.

The day arrived. I picked Lisa up and we drove to the garden;
she did not know in advance where we were going. We made our way
through several different areas in the gorgeous place, taking a few 3D
pictures here and there. At a spot with a large boulder, I suggested we
stop for awhile. I set up my camera on a tripod and I turned on my jam
box, tuned to the correct station. That may have been the only thing that

seemed awry to Lisa; we never listened to the hard rock station.

We sat next to each other on the boulder, enjoYing the beautiful day and the perfect environment around us. I handed the radio to Lisa because I knew the time was getting close. As one song was fading out, the female deejay's voice was heard: "And now, here's a special song for Lisa, from Mike."

*The Question, Popped* swelled from the speakers. Once the intro was over, my voice began, and Lisa recognized that it was me.

> I've told you my life story,
> My triumphs and my crimes.
> I've told you that I love you
> At least a thousand times.
> You've heard my wild ambitions;
> I've shared my hopes and dreams.
> With all the things I've told you,
> You've heard it all, it seems.
> But I hope you'll listen to just one thing more…
> Something you never heard me say before:
> Will you marry me?
> You know I've been waiting all my life.
> And there's no way I'll be content
> Until you say you'll be my wife.
> Will you marry me?

There's a bridge and a second verse, but you get the picture, right? Oh, and speaking of pictures, my 3D camera captured the moment as Lisa realized it was me on the radio. At the end of the song, there's one final "Will you marry me?" and then there's the sound of wedding bells.

As the song ended, I dropped to one knee and pulled a ring from my pocket. "What do you say?"

She said yes.

The deejay came back on the air and explained what was going on, that I'd written and recorded this song and that when she learned the outcome, she would report it to the listeners. Lisa and I walked up to the clubhouse (yep, this was pre-cellphone times) and called the station.

We've had 26 anniversaries since then. How many times have we told that story? Beats me. But it always elicits a big response. Women usually sigh contentedly and men often say, "Thanks for setting the bar so high, dude."

Is my life better because of how I proposed?

You better believe it. We had a Technicolor proposal and have had a wonderful marriage and an amazing daughter and many, many adventures…and it all grew out of that thrilling idea, made possible by the skill I already possessed and the drill I'd put in.

And if you'd like to hear the song and see the picture of this moment, here's a link to a hidden page on my website:

http://bit.do/popped.
Or just scan the QR code below.

# 6.

# JUST LIKE ADAM & EVE

Okay, so being creative can help you in your personal life. But what about in your career, your professional existence? I thought you'd never ask.

Not long after Lisa and I got married, I had an unpleasant feeling.

I was stuck.

Have you ever felt stuck in your job? You feel so unfulfilled and unhappy, but you don't know what alternative you have.

That's where I was.

I was working at a small church, leading the music and working with the teenagers, and I'd been doing it for over four years.

I was burned out. Yes, I know, it's hard to believe that you could ever get tired of working with teenagers, right? But I can confirm that it is indeed possible. I was drained. Plus, hanging around students was not nearly as exciting as it was before I had a beautiful young wife waiting for me at home.

I needed a change, but what else could I do? What skills did I have that would be useful in the secular world?

I could direct a choir. But Exxon and AT&T and IBM didn't have choirs, did they?

I could drive the church van. But I didn't want to be a bus driver.

Grasping for answers, I looked around our little house, and there was one possibility, sitting on a desk in the living room.

Shortly after we got married, we did something crazy, something unnecessary.

We bought a computer.

This was long ago, my children, in an age when I did not know a single other person who owned a personal comPuter. In 1987, they were still exotic and rare, and there really wasn't a good reason for me to buy one.

Except I saw my first Mac. While browsing in a computer store, I saw the usual monitors with green DOS letters spelling out secret commands. But then the sales guy showed me the Mac Classic, one of those one-piece beige boxes with the handle and the tiny little black and white screen. This computer looked different; the screen was clean and white. The sales guy showed me how to use a tool to draw a circle on the screen. Then he clicked a little paint bucket tool and the circle was filled with a checkerboard pattern.

I was charmed.

I bought that Mac and took it home and began learning about it.

We didn't even buy a hard drive at first, which meant endlessly swapping diskettes to save a document. I started using the Mac to do flyers and newsletters for my church job and it turned out that I had a real affinity for what was then called "desktop publishing."

Looking at that Mac in our living room, I thought, "What if I could find somebody to pay me to do desktop publishing? Hmmm." At that moment, that was the only skill I felt I could use to get unstuck from the fix I was in. It *was* a skill, though; it was *something*.

I had done plenty of drill work, too. With typical newbie zeal, I had checked out every library book on desktop publishing. I collected fonts from any source I could find. I studied books on designing logos. I even had a gizmo to scan photos...at home...in 1987! It was called a ThunderScan; look it up, you'll be amazed at the bizarre method it used.

Where could I find a job to use these skills? I had an idea. In the late 1980s, fanzines—or just "zines"—were a huge trend, and I had begun publishing a zine of my own, which I'll tell you about later. To have my zine printed, I had started frequenting a copy shop, one that was part of a chain of about six stores in town. Maybe they would like to hire a desktop publishing semi-expert.

At the corporate office for the printing chain, I filled out their standard employee application and I went home and sat by the phone.

For three days.

It never rang.

By this time, dear reader, you should know what I was missing. I had the skill and had done the drill, but...where was the thrilling idea?

Since I hadn't received any response after three days, I decided I needed to kick things into a higher gear. I set to work and soon finished a four-page newsletter.

About me.

It was even called *The Robertson Reader*, and in the course of its four pages, it showed that I could set nice columns of type just like a real magazine. It showed that I could design logos, scan photographs, lay out pages, and write good copy. There was a list of all the software programs in which I had become proficient. My employment history was on the back page, along with a list of all the reasons why I would be the best employee this company had ever hired.

After printing several copies of the newsletter, I returned to the corporate office and approached the front desk.

"May I help you?" the receptionist asked.

"Yes, ma'am," I replied. "I'd like to drop this off and I would be glad to wash the car or shine the shoes of anyone in this company." I don't know where that thought came from, but when I said it, I saw heads popping up above cubicles and curious faces wanting to get a look at this oddball. Nobody stepped forward to claim a car wash or a shoeshine, but I would have provided either if given the chance.

Instead, I went back home. Three hours later, the phone rang.

The president of the printing company was calling. She said, "I can see that I need to meet you. Can you come in tomorrow afternoon?"

Absolutely, I said.

On the following day, I sat in her office as she looked fondly at *The Robertson Reader*. "I love what you've done here. But we don't have a position available for what you want to do…"

Long pause.

"But I do have an idea." Boy, did I wanna hear what her idea was.

"I've thought for a long time how great it would be if a business owner were to come into our store and say, 'I need a logo and business cards and letterhead,' and then he could sit down next to a designer and watch as all those things were designed and walk out of the store with a finished product. Do you think you could do that? While-you-wait graphic design?"

Absolutely, I said.

I had no idea if I could do it or not, but when the brass ring comes around, you gotta grab it, right?

The following week, I became the first while-you-wait graphic designer in Austin. It was incredibly challenging to have a person sitting next to me, paying by the hour, while I whipped up logos, newsletter, flyers, cassette covers, t-shirt designs, and many other projects. I became much better as a designer and much speedier at filling requests. After a year and a haLf, I left the printing company and opened my own graphic design business.

Let's pause here to examine what happened.

I was stuck. I applied at *one* company. For a job *that did not exist*. And they created a position for me that put me on the cutting edge of the digital revolution that would completely transform the printing business. I got to be a pioneer.

Just like Adam and Eve, my life was dramatically changed forever by an Apple.

But that's not all. That desktop publishing job was the last job application I ever filled out. Every job I've had since then has come to me because someone saw what I could do and said, "How would you like to come do that for us…for more money?"

Skill + Drill + Thrill is a potent combination. I'm living proof.

Twenty years after I did *The Robertson Reader*, I was delighted to see that my daughter had done something similar. She was in college and learned that a LUSH cosmetics store was going to be opening up in Austin. Lindsey had been a fan of LUSH products, but we had only been able to find them when we traveled to other cities. She was pleased that there would be a local LUSH and she decided that's where she wanted to work.

Before the store even opened, Lindsey prepared her resume. She was already quite familiar with their product line, and she knew that their stores featured small signs on all their products; the signs were made to look like blackboards and the product info was written in a white font that looked like chalk marks. Lindsey duplicated this look in the design of her resume and I'm convinced that is what got the attention of the store manager. She worked there for her last two years of college and then, when she moved to New York City to pursue an acting career, she easily found work in two of the NYC LUSH stores.

She only applied to one place, did her research, came up with a cool idea, and got the result she wanted.

That's my girl!

# 7.

# PLEASE PERUSE THIS
# PARTICULARLY PERTINENT PARABLE

You awaken in a white room. All the furnishings are white. You rise and walk through other rooms, all equally white and featureless. You have no memory, no knowledge of anything except your own existence and the existence of your environment. There are no windows, no books, no television. But there are cushioned chairs, carpeted floors, a comfortable bed.

You are a blank slate. With no previous knowledge or memories, you are experiencing everything for the first time. The feel of the carpet, the temperature of the air, the realization of the body you inhabit.

After a few hours, you begin to feel something, a twinge in the middle of your body and a feeling that you need something. You don't know the word "hunger," but that's what you're experiencing.

And then you smell something. The air is different. You swivel your head around and move through the rooms. In one room is a white table which you examined earlier. But now there is something on the table.

Something round. Flat. And your nostrils flare with the scent of the thing you cannot name.

It's a cheese pizza. But even if you heard those words, they wouldn't mean anything to you.

You reach towards the round, flat object. You can feel its warmth. The aroma is causing your mouth to salivate and you swAllow unconsciously, stirred instinctively to explore further.

You put your face very close to the pizza and something in your brain tells you to taste it. So you lift one edge of the pizza and gingerly take a small bite. A charge courses through your body as every cell in you cheers and says "More!" You take a larger bite and chew it, aware of the flavors radiating through you.

You eat until you are full and you are aware that you have learned something. Twinge in stomach = cured by object on table.

Hours go by and you again feel the growling in your midsection and when you go to the table, there is another cheese pizza.

This becomes your routine. You sleep, you explore the white rooms, and two or three times a day, you feel hunger and go to the table to find another cheese pizza has materialized. For weeks, this happens dependably.

And then one day you approach the table and something is different. There's a round, flat thing there, but it has little circular things on top of it. You're not happy about your normal routine being disrupted, but you lean close to the pizza and can smell something a bit different. You pull one of the circular things from the top of the cheese, sniff it, touch it with your tongue and then taste it.

Now your world includes pepperoni pizza. You were satisfied

before, but now things seem even better. Over the next few weeks, you're never quite sure what will appear on the table. Sometimes it's a cheese pizza; sometimes it's a pepperoni pizza. And sometimes there are other things on the pizza. You like them all and you look forward to each meal to see what variation you'll be getting this time.

Months later, you approach the table because it's hungry time. But there is no pizza there. Instead, there is a small, spherical object, flecked with orange, yellow and red. What is this? You examine it. It's not hot to the touch. It's sort of…fuzzy. You hold it to your nose and sniff and your eyes go wide. This is different. You gather your courage and decide to bite into it because you are so hungry.

And your tastebuds go crazy as the flavor of this ripe peach explodes and the scent is intoxicating and the juice is running down your chin and all you can think is, "Where has this thing been?"

You thought you knew about food. Oh, sometimes there was cheese and sometimes pepperoni and sometimes mushrooms…but nothing prepared you for a fresh peach. Again, you have learned something.

Life continues, but now the variety in your diet is like a game. Each time you head to the room with the table, you wonder what you will find? The pizza? The peach?

Until the day when you see something completely different on your white table. It's not round and flat. It's…different. You reach out to touch it, to examine it, and you are startled when it jerks away from your touch. You notice that the sides of this…thing…are moving in and out, just like your own ribs do when you breathe. You reach again and feel the furry back…the rubbery flippers…

You're ahead of me, aren't you? Yes, that duck-billed platypus has finally showed up.

This little story is an oversimplification of how we all face life. We find a routine that becomes familiar and comforting and most of us are content to stay right there, living a cheese pizza life. We often will not vary from that routine unless circumstances force us to. Maybe we will get adventurous and try the pepperoni.

But imagine that person (you) in the white room. Imagine thinking life was all pizza and then one day experiencing a peach. Could you go back? I hope not. Once we experience that next level of knowledge, our eyes open a little bit wider and we have become wiser. But no matter how many peaches we may eat, nothing prepares us to come face-to-bill with a platypus. Even scientists were perplexed when the platypus was first sighted.

For the person in the white room, the platypus is mind-blowing and yields some life-changing ideas. Not everything is for eating! Something else is alive besides me!

And most importantly: What else is out there?

That's the question you should never stop asking, regardless of your age, your achievements, or your level of contentment. Asking "What else is out there?" doesn't mean you're dissatisfied. It means you're open to new amazement, that you have progressed to a new height.

My two favorite television shows of all time are *Twin Peaks* and *Lost*. Both were quirky dramas with large casts and complicated stories. And both ended in ways that many people found unsatisfying. I was not among that group.

J.J. Abrams, the creator of *Lost*, gave a now-famous speech at a

TED conference a few years ago; if you by chance have not seen it, look it up online and enjoy. He tells about buying a "mystery box" at a magic store when he was a teenager. The box promised fifty dollars worth of magic tricks for fifteen bucks, but it was a grab bag. You didn't get to look in the box before buying it. J.J. showed the box to the TED audience, telling them that he still kept it in his office, decades later, and that he had never opened it. Never.

He credited a large part of his very-successful career to the fact that he had never opened the mystery box. He believed that a sealed box offered infinite possibilities, while an opened box only had one.

I love that so much. As a person who's spent major portions of my life in church, I know that the most dissatisfied people in the world are those who think they should have all the answers.

Guess what? You don't get 'em. Nobody has all the answers, and if you meet someone who claims to, hold tight to your wallet and walk rapidly in the opposite direction.

Watching *Lost* and *Twin Peaks* helped me come to the place in my life where I could let go of the need to know it all. Instead, I found the joy of knowing a few things…and the unspeakable excitement of not having any idea what else might be out there.

The CPPs (Cheese Pizza People) of the world think they've seen it all. They're going to miss out on so much. Not just peaches and platypuses…but pineapples and papayas, pickles and pork rinds, Paris and parasailing.

Don't put up with the prosaic when you can ponder the prodigious.

Pretty please.

# 8.

# WHO'S ON FIRST

Which is most important: the skill, the drill, or the thrill?

For me, the answer changes. For a long time, I believed that having the skill, the talent, was the main thing. Then I became convinced that the thrill was the biggest factor in the equation. I often shortchanged the drill part, but I now know that it is crucial for achieving a satisfying, creative, successful life.

Because you have to be ready.

Opportunity does not send you a letter that says, "Hi, there, in seven weeks I'll be showing up to give you a wonderful chance to do something marvelous."

It jumps out of the bushes and scares you half to death.

It usually doesn't give any advance notice at all.

I remember a story I read while in college, forty *choke* years ago. It concerned one of my favorite rock bands, an English group called the Who.

The Who were not yet at the superstar level they would eventually attain. They had recorded a new album and were going on a US tour which would be very important to the sales of that record and to building the reputation of the band.

On the second night of the tour, the Who was at the Cow Palace in San Francisco. They took the stage and played some of their hits before launching into their new album. But it became clear that something was amiss on the stage.

Keith Moon, the drummer for the Who, was a notorious bad boy/wild man of rock and roll, infamous for the wholesale destruction of hotel rooms, driving a Rolls Royce into a swimming pool, and ingesting anything that promised to deliver an interesting experience. He had ingested something on this night that caused him to collapse behind his drum kit in mid-song and fall backward onto the stage.

The music came to a halt, as roadies came out from the wings, gathered Keith up and dragged him backstage, where they put him in a cold shower for several minutes.

The audience waited for half an hour before the band once again came onstage and started to play, but Moon's recovery was only momentary and within minutes he again blacked out behind the drums.

Pete Townshend, the Who's legendary guitarist and songwriter, was furious at Moon for disrupting this important concert and the premiere of his new collection of songs. As the roadies again dragged Keith offstage, Pete stepped to the microphone, looked across the crowded auditorium and said, "Can anybody play the drums? I mean somebody good!"

In the audience was a 19-year-old kid named Scot Halpin, who had played drums with a few local bands. His friend began pointing at Scot and yelling, "He can play! He can play!" In truth, it had been over a year since Scot had done any drumming, but when members of the crew asked him if he could indeed do this, he said yes.

Moments later, Scot Halpin was seated behind Keith Moon's drum kit, and Pete Townshend was saying Scot should waTch him for cues.

And the band began to play. And Scot played the rest of the concert as the drummer of one of the best rock groups in the world. At nineteen, he was plucked out of the crowd because he said "Yes," when opportunity very unexpectedly presented itself.

I was nineteen when I read that story. Do you know how jealous I was of Scot Halpin? Even though I wasn't a drummer? It was every wannabe rock star's fantasy come true. I have been to so many Beach Boys concerts, just waiting for a moment when someone onstage would say, "Can anybody out there sing Brian Wilson's part?"

Hasn't happened…yet.

But I'm ready. That's the key, being ready. Scot Halpin didn't attend that concert with any intention or even any hope of playing with the Who; what a crazy idea! But when the question was asked, "Can you do this?" he simply said yes. Because of years spent banging on the drums in nameless garage bands, he had enough of a reason to accept this chance. He'd done the drill. He didn't even have the thrilling idea himself; it came from his friend and the road crew and Pete Townshend…and even from Keith Moon.

How many times have you had a choice to make between doing what you've always done and trying something scary yet life-changing?

We all get such chances, but most of us unfortunately say no.

"I'll stick with the cheese pizza; it's fine."

And you add another page to your life story that just says, "Ditto."

Just like yesterday.

And the day before.

Instead, try saying yes. You may discover something that changes your life in a phenomenal way.

Who knows? The Who knows.

# 9.

# **DISPENSING WITH NORMALCY**

I mentioned in a previous chapter that I published a zine in the late 80s. Even that was an example of finding my own path and doing something creative.

Do you recognize the item pictured here?

It's a PEZ candy dispenser. When you push back the head of the cartoon character, a little candy brick pops out.

PEZ dispensers became popular in the USA in the 1950s, about the same time I made my first appearance in the USA. I remember having PEZ dispensers as a child and liking them, even though the candy is not especially tasty. The dispensers were cool.

Years went by and I was a freshman in college when my roommate and I went into a Woolworth's store and saw PEZ for sale. In a burst of nostalgia, I bought a couple of the dispensers; they were just twentY-five cents each. This time, though, I hung on to them. I soon bought others and began to make a habit of looking for them.

Before long, I knew every store that sold PEZ and had acquired a couple dozen different dispensers. I wrote to the PEZ company and received a photocopied list of all the dispensers they had ever sold. There were many I did not have, but for years I searched, adding a few new ones each year. I never knew another person who collected PEZ, though I figured there had to be others.

In the 1980s I began reading a publication called *The Toy Shop*. It was a tabloid filled with hundreds of classified ads, and I pored over each issue, hoping to find another person who had an interest in these plastic doohickeys.

And one day, I did. I didn't find just one person, either; two people had placed ads in the magazine saying they were interested in trading or buying PEZ dispensers. I wrote to both of them and soon made a couple of trades, swapping duplicates from my collection for dispensers I'd never seen before. One of these collectors told me about a zine about toys that was published by a guy in Northern California; this fellow collected PEZ, too, and frequently mentioned them in his zine.

I fired off a letter to him and soon was receiving his publication. After I'd received a few issues, I was able to write an article that he printed in the zine and I felt a thrill of being (sort of) in print. Before long, I had a regular column and was designing the magazine cover on my handy new Mac.

The publisher, though, informed me that he had decided to stop putting out his zine. He offered to sell it to me, for much more than I could have spent. Instead, I told him, I was thinking about doing my own zine, completely devoted to PEZ. I asked him how many PEZ collectors he thought there were in the United States. He estimated thirty or forty.

That was enough for me. I started designing my first zine, spending hours tinkering with the layout, the articles, the pictures, even the name. I ultimately decided to call it *The Optimistic Pezzimist*. I placed a classified ad in *The Toy Shop*, announcing the first issue and asking for subscriptions.

The next few days passed slowly as I waited for mail to arrive. But then I got my first subscription, then another and another. By the time I printed the first issue, I had more than 40 subscribers. I stuffed zines into envelopes and licked every one of them. I was a publisher.

The first issue of *OP*, as it came to be called, was a hit. Unlike most of the cut-and-paste zines of the time, it had a clean-looking layout and more information about PEZ than had ever been assembled in one place. That first issue won an editor's choice award from a newsstand magazine that reviewed hundreds of zines each issue, and that prompted more people to write and subscribe.

Life became very interesting. My mailbox would be stuffed almost every day with great things: letters from all over the world, dispensers I had bought or traded for, photos that subscribers sent to show their prized collectibles.

The subscriber list grew and grew. Within a year, I had over 400 subscribers, at eighteen dollars each. My little hobby turned out to be much bigger than anyone had ever imagined and there were PEZ collectors everywhere.

I got phone calls, too. *People* magazine. *The Wall Street Journal.*

*Supermarket Sweep*, the TV game show. *Playboy*! The Canadian Broadcasting Company wanted to interview me. I became the go-to person for information on PEZ. Even the PEZ company began referring queries to me.

There was so much interest that I decided there should be a convention for PEZ collectors. I put together the plans and set the date, and the First PEZ Dispens-O-Rama was held in Cleveland, where dozens of PEZ-heads got to meet their peers for the first time. Rare items were sold and traded, both in the vendor room and in the hotel rooms upstairs. We had an auction at which I made my best sale ever. I auctioned one PEZ dispenser—which I had purchased for a quarter—and it went for six hundred dollars!

Two weeks later, my daughter was born. Instead of cigars, I handed out girl PEZ dispensers.

I had created a subculture and the resultant interest caused PEZ prices to skyrocket. Where collectors had once fretted over paying four dollars for a dispenser, now many of them were selling for triple digits.

When that many people are trying to get the best stuff, however, things inevitably get ugly. I began hearing of some collectors cheating others, of newly-discovered collections that were procured in sneaky ways, and I even learned of some counterfeit PEZ dispensers. The president of the PEZ company threatened to sue me if I infringed on their copyrights (I had not). Subscribers began to complain about any changes or delays in the zine. And at my house, there was an adorable little baby girl who merited my attention more than my computer and my collection did.

I planned my exit from the PEZ world. I divided my collection into several groups and held a series of phone auctions, getting rid of almost all of my PEZ memorabilia, which had appreciated greatly in value largely due to the collector interest generated by my magazine. I netted thousands of dollars from the sale of my collection.

With that money, I bought my freedom, in more than one way. The phone calls and letters and requests for interviews gradually slowed to a stop. But with the profits from my auctions, I purchased a brand new Mac, a scanner, a laser printer, and I quit my job with the printing company, opening my own graphic design business.

Following the formula once again, my skills in writing and desktop publishing were combined with the thrilling idea of putting out my own little magazine. But it was the drill, the years of gradually building both my collection and my knowledge, that ultimately brought me a certain measure of fame, financial return, and the freedom to begin my own business.

Can something as small as a PEZ dispenser change the whole direction of a person's life? I think you know what my answer is.

Mike Robertson

# 10.

# THIS AIN'T NO PARTY

Once you switch on your creative pipeline, you'll begin to find ways to use your creativity that you never considered before, even ways that you might think don't need creative solutions.

Or have you forgotten? There's *always* more.

Lisa and I have one child, a daughter named Lindsey. We didn't plan to have just one kid, but that's how things happened. Fortunately, we got it right the first time and Lindsey was a delight from the moment she came into our lives.

If you have children, you have probably had your share of birthday parties. Things have definitely changed since I was a child; I only remember having one party. My mother was always great at making special cakes and giving perfect gifts, but parties were not as prevalent back then. And the concept of giving every child a goodie bag full of toys and treats did not exist back then; if it had, I might not have had even that one party, because Mom had a very small budget.

Lindsey's first two or three birthdays were quiet, home-based celebrations. But when she was four, we knew we had to do better. I'm sorry to say that we didn't make a very creative decision; we went to Chuck E. Cheese.

The party there was okay, but I felt there was something missing. It was not a personalized experience. In fact, there were three or four other parties going on right there in the same room where the giant rat performed with his animatronic pals.

For birthday number five, we decided to create our own celebration. As always, the first step was to look around at what skill or tools we had on hand. One thing we had was a red, white and blue footlocker that I'd bought to take to my first year of college, more than twenty years earlier. But it was the contents of the trunk that provided an inspiration.

When Lisa and I were dating, we were both active in a community theater group. Both of us had acted, directed, built sets, and put together costumes. Inside the red, white and blue trunk were all the outfits Lisa had gathered for theater productions: a prom dress from the early 1960s, old bridesmaid dresses, hats, shoes, all sorts of things.

Our daughter loved to play dress-up using the contents of this trunk and we figured that most other little girls liked that, too.

Okay, that's a start. What else?

Lisa's mother had a beautiful swimming pool in her backyard. Lindsey loved to splash around in the water and her grandma loved having her there.

That was what we had to work with, a trunk full of costumes and a swimming pool.

From that, we created the Splashin' Fashion party. A half-dozen little girls came to the party and they had a blast rummaging through all the fancy clothes, picking out hats and jewelry.

Out by the pool, I had set up a little sound system. I'd found some old music suitable for fashion shows. As the little girls came out, one at a time, they paraded around the pool like runway models while I described their ensembles in glowing terms. After they comPleted the circuit, they raced back into the house to pick out a new outfit.

The moms of all these girls were charmed by our idea, applauding and laughing as the kids clomped around in high heels and long dresses. Once everyone had modeled several things, they all went and put on their swimsuits and we got to the splashin' part of the party.

It was a modest start that cost almost nothing, but it drew high compliments from all the kids and mothers. And it told us we were doing something good by creating original party ideas.

The following year, we had a party at the zoo, which was fun, but not especially creative, so we vowed to get back to the original stuff.

By age seven, Lindsey was into slumber parties. Consequently, one of her parties was a mystery/detective party at our house in the country. In the goodie bag each girl received was a little notepad, a magnifying glass, a Sherlock Holmes-style bubble pipe, a flashlight and some other items. They were told that the birthday piñata had been stolen and their job was to find it. But how?

Lindsey always wanted a giant cookie instead of a cake. When we cut the cookie, a clue was revealed underneath it. The girls had to get together and decipher the clue, which led them to the next one. One clue required them to turn to certain pages in a giant dictionary and look for a highlighted word on each page. Those words combined to find another clue. It was dark outside by now, but the clue said they should dig in a designated spot in the garden. They found a small leather bag with gold coins and a clue about following a scarlet thread. Near the front porch, they found a strand of red yarn and they began to follow it out into the trees, lit only by their little flashlights.

There were squeals and occasional screams, but the girls were completely into the hunt by now. The red yarn led them a hundred yards through the trees, away from the house to a campfire. Seated by the fire was a cackling gypsy woman with a witchy nose and a warty chin. Yep, I told you my wife had theatrical experience. The girls argued among themselves over who would hand the coins over to the crone. When it was done they received another clue.

I can't remember all the clues from that evening, but I do recall that we had the most excited group of girls I'd ever seen. They could not stop talking about their detective adventure and when the parents arrived next morning, they launched into their favorite parts all over again.

It was so much fun that I couldn't wait for the next year!

We decided that we would make a movie during the next party. I wrote a simple script and, when the girls arrived, we let them pick their parts and put together their costumes. I directed them through each scene while Lisa videotaped them. It was hilarious fun, especially when one of the girls would use an accent or try to act like an arch-villain.

Once we had enough footage, the girls devoured the cookie and other refreshments, while I loaded the footage into my iMac and began to edit it together in the first version of iMovie. I stayed up all night, adding music and credits, and putting some of the bloopers and crack-ups at the end of the seven-minute spy movie. Then I made a VHS copy (yes, it was before DVDs) for each girl. They were all asleep on the living room floor long before I was finished.

The following morning, we watched the movie and their laughter and joy was a thrill to behold. Once again, the parents who arrived could not believe what we had done.

As Lindsey got older, we tried to make each year's party something special. On her twelfth birthday, we decided to make a music video. We shot video of the girls, solo and as a group, lip-syncing to "What I Like About You." I added some MTV-style shots where they all jumped into the air at the same time, or laid on the floor with their heads together, singing the song. There was even a shot where they all smiled, revealing joke teeth I had bought. Once again, I stayed up all night, editing the video, and ended up with a great product.

During the year when *The DaVinci Code* was a huge bestseller, we did DaLinzi Code. The girl met at a prearranged location and found a stretch white limousine waiting. Then they were handed a mysterious clue. They had to solve the clue so they could tell the driver where to take them. At one stop, they all received t-shirts with a photo on the front of the Mona Lisa, with Lindsey's face substituted. They all wore their shirts for the other stops on the hunt, including one at the mall.

These treasure hunt parties were so much fun that I later did similar activities for a group of adults. Six teams of four or five people showed up to chase around Austin for some missing artifact. I made some very complicated clues for these hunts; I would walk through a craft store like Hobby Lobby or Michaels and look for things that seemed to have good potential: tiny wooden boxes, Scrabble letter tiles, old-looking blank books…there were so many possibilities. And I would buy paint kits to make a wooden box look like rusted iron or copper with a green patina. The clues were much better because I took the time to make them look like something from a movie, instead of just handing out slips of paper.

I learned, time after time, that if I planned a party I would enjoy attending, the chances were good that others would love them, too. Instead of having friends over and just standing around talking and drinking, try giving them a mystery to solve or a treasure to find. They will never forget it.

How long has it been since you went on a treasure hunt? Well, that's too long. *That's why I've hidden a clue in this book which can lead you to a treasure. If you're very observant, you may already have seen a couple of things which you thought were mistakes. There may indeed be some mistakes, but there are also some on-purpose oddities scattered throughout the pages. Once I wrote this chapter and remembered those treasure hunts, I thought it would be a capital idea to plant some clues for you, too. Good luck! Oh, and there's a little clue in this paragraph, too.*

# 11.

# A NEW WAY TO GO

Can traveling be done in a creative way? Of course! You should know by this point that *everything* can be done in a creative way.

Our vacations used to revolve around shopping and sightseeing. There's nothing wrong with that, but if you're committed to buying souvenirs whenever you travel, you're going to wake up one day and realize you have a lot of useless knick-knacks which either need dusting constantly or are stuck in boxes where they provide no return on your investment and can't really impact your life.

And what about photographs? They either take up space in photo albums (which also require dusting) or they occupy space on your computer hard drive, thousands of shots that you hardly ever look at.

So what's the element of traveling that will last? It's the encounters with people and the times you did something out of the ordinary.

I started learning this lesson by necessity on my honeymoon. I had very little money, so it was completely out of the question to go to

Hawaii or take a cruise or travel to Europe after our wedding. My bank account told me I was going to be honeymooning in Texas.

Still, I wanted to do some things that would be romantic and memorable. I thought it would be fun for us to travel around the state, staying in bed-and-breakfast inns. In those pre-internet days, that meant I had to do research at the library and the bookstore, looking for B&Bs that sounded charming and were reasonably priced. Then I mapped out a roUte which included several of the inns I'd picked.

It turned out to be a wonderful time for Lisa and I. We covered lots of miles, listening to great music, seeing the back roads, and meeting some great people. We stayed one night at a place called The Pink Lady, a Victorian house in Bastrop, Texas, where the innkeepers were an older couple. The husband loaded us into a Model T Ford and chauffeured us around town, keeping up a steady stream of corny jokes.

Each inn had its own personality and we enjoyed them all. On Saturday night, we were staying in a small town outside of Houston and we decided that we would go to church the next morning at an African-American church in the big city. After a huge breakfast prepared by the earth-mother-innkeeper, we dressed up in our going-away outfits. Lisa's ensemble included a hat with a veil. My double-breasted suit was accompanied by spats on my shoes. We found the church and went inside. We were the only white people in the place. It felt like home, though, because the choir was singing a song that was on the tape player in our car. I sang along, which caused some sur-prised looks in the congregation.

The service was long, but we loved every minute of it. And it only got better afterward. When the members of the church found out we were on our honeymoon, they invited us to stay for lunch, asked to hear about our wedding, and even gave us t-shirts with a picture of the church on the front.

Kind of an odd thing to do on a honeymoon, huh?

Exactly! That's the idea! Do something new, something that broadens your horizons a bit. Look for what will make an interesting story in your life book.

Each Sunday morning, I teach two classes at my church. I've been doing it for eight years and both classes have been very well-attended, largely, I think, because of my constant search to do something new and creative and non-churchy. I think I can say that those two classes love me a great deal. Last Christmas, they proved it.

I had never been overseas before. I always wanted to, but the opportunity and the funding never seemed to come together. I apparently mentioned in class one day that I would love to go to London. I don't even remember saying that, but someone latched onto that information and filed it away and began to organize a little project.

Just before Christmas, I was starting the second class of the day when I saw the members of class number one filing into the room. Hmmm.

That's when they told me that they were sending Lisa and me to England. They presented us a Harrod's shopping bag filled with maps and books and one-pound coins and Walker's Shortbread…

and a substantial check. They had wisely decided not to plan our trip, because they know I'm such a researcher and planner myself. But they had given us enough money for us to plan without having to skimp.

Lisa and I decided to take the train from London to Paris while we were in the neighborhood and I began looking for cool things to do. My classes were excited because they knew I would return with many new stories and experiences to share. They have learned—as I hope you have—that stories are incredibly powerful and important.

London and Paris…how could I decide what to do in these amazing cities? I tried thinking of ways to interact with people, since I knew that's where the best stories come from.

We wanted to take a tour of London in one of their black cabs. But I found a cab which was painted like a black and white Holstein cow. I knew we had to try the Cow Cab, especially since it was a one-man operation, not a large company. Sure enough, the driver of the cab was a friendly guy named Steve. We tried to find out as much about him as he found out about us. He showed us the sights, snapped pictures of us whenever we wanted to stop, and bravely stood in the middle of the street while Lisa and I crossed Abbey Road in the footsteps of the Beatles. While driving us about, Steve pointed out a restaurant and said, "There's the second-best fish and chips shop in London."

I had to ask, "Well, where's the *first* best?" He took us there. That's where we ate our first dinner in London. Before Steve left us, I had him speak to my classes back in Texas on video, and even got him to say, "Howdy, y'all."

When I learned we were going to England, I thought, "Wouldn't it be great if I could speak at a church in London?" I'll spare you the details, but it happened! Oh, I got turned down by the first church I asked, but the second one said yes, and we had the most charming day getting to know the people at the Northolt Grange Baptist Church. We were invited to have tea and cakes after the service and even given a ride back to our hotel by a church member.

And all I had to do to make that dream come true was ask! What could you accomplish if you were willing to ask someone to help fulfill your dream?

When I think about it, the fact that I was turned down by the first church I approached is a reminder of the first radio station I approached to play my propoSal song. If you give up on your dream because one person tells you "No," you're probably not going to make that dream a reality. Don't take rejection as the final answer. There is a "Yes" out there somewhere…probably out there on the border between platypus and Technicolor.

Several years ago, we were planning our first trip to DisneyWorld. Lindsey was a teenager by then and invited my sister's daughter to go along with us; these cousins were born only three months apart and have always had great fun together.

I knew we would have fun at Disney, but I wanted to make some extra-special memories on this trip. Walt Disney himself used to ask his Imagineers to find ways to "plus" the experience for visitors, to give them more than they expected.

It occurred to me that, out of the millions of people who visit a

Disney park each year, most were only concerned with getting their money's worth and being treated well. I like that, too, but I started thinking, "What if we set out to be the best guests at DisneyWorld?" How could we make the Disney employees— or "cast members" — feel special?

I had some ideas, and I once again called on my graphic design skills to make them reality.

I designed some Disney-themed thank-you letters for the house-keeping staff—er, Mousekeepers—at our hotel, one for each day of our stay. The letters featured Disney character art and were even printed in a font that looked like Walt Disney's handwriting.

Then, using a button-making gizmo I found at a craft store, I made some round pinback badges which had a photo of our family and bore the legend: "You've been selected Cast Member of the Day by the Robertson family from Texas." When I would give one of these to a Disney worker who had been especially nice or helpful to us, their faces would light up and they would immediately pin the badge on their vest.

It cost almost nothing, but added so many wonderful memories to our trip.

But my fondest memory of that trip was when a couple of cast members "plussed" our Magic Kingdom stay in a most magical way.

It was late evening, only an hour or so before the park would be closing. We had planned to see the Main Street Electrical Parade, which featured lots of floats and characters adorned with colorful lights, a parade which had to be done after dark.

Thanks to my research, I had learned that a good place to watch the parade was away from the crowded Main Street; instead we found a spot back by Liberty Square. As I mentioned, we had two teenage girls and they were soon spotted by a couple of young male cast members who were setting up the rope stanchions before the parade began. The boys talked to Lindsey and Maeghan, asking where they were from, what they'd seen that day, etc.

But then one of the boys held his hands out in front of him, cupped together as though he were carrying water or sand. He stood in front of the girls and told them he had some pixie dust and he wanted them both to blow it into the air when he counted to three.

They giggled, of course, but they moved close together as the boy raised his hands toward their faces.

"Ready?" he said. "One...two...THREE!" The girls puffed as though there were birthday candles in front of them.

And every light in the entire park went out. At that instant.

It's all a matter of timing, of course, of knowing the music that plays each night and when it signals that the parade is about to begin.

But magic almost always depends on timing, doesn't it? It depends on knowing the drill.

That little incident has stuck in my mind more than any ride, any meal, any show we saw at DisneyWorld.

Why?

Because it set off my sense of wonder. And there's nothing I like more than that.

Next time you go on a trip, pause and ask yourself what you want to achieve on this journey. Buying stuff? Seeing stuff? Doing stuff?

Instead, look for the wonder. Put yourself in places that have the ability to surprise you. Find a hotel that's not part of a chain. Eat at the local favorite restaurant. And look for opportunities to evoke wonder in someone else. You'll never forget or regret it.

# 12.

# SIZE MATTERS

There have been times in my life when I had a weight problem... and I'm not talking about anorexia; I kicked that one to the curb long ago. On my birth certificate, it proclaims that "Baby Robertson" was born weighing 9 lbs, 10 ounces.

Nine pounds, ten ounces. From the second I was born I had a weight problem! Don't tell me it's not genetic! As a result, I am a veteran of the diet wars, having pledged my allegiance to many different regimens, all of which promised to make me into a Greek god. I *think* there was a Greek god named Humongous, wasn't there?

My first diet was in the 1970s, when I endured something called the liquid protein diet. It was also commonly referred to as the liquid death diet, since several people died while using it. The diet involved drinking a couple of tablespoons of a thick, supposedly-cherry-flavored liquid three times a day. This liquid was made by boiling down cowhides, so you can imagine how great it tasted.

Did I lose weight? I sure did; laboratory rats got more and better rations than I got. I lost weight.

Did I gain it all back? Yes, and then some.

On to the next. I tried the Cambridge Diet, the Atkins diet, the South Beach diet. I've done low-fat. I've done low-cal. I've done low-carb. I went lo-co! I've learned, though, that I can lose weight on just about any diet. The problem is that I can *gain* weight by watching a Dairy Queen commercial.

Even if you are successful in dieting, that presents its own set of problems. At one point I had been dieting for several months and had reached the lowest weight I'd been since high school, so I needed new clothes. Being a cheapskate, I went to a men's resale shop, although one which only accepted high-quality items. I found several things I liked but then I came upon something really nice: a navy blazer, double-breasted, with lapels so wide that they were in different time zones from one another. I looked at the label insiDe and it said "YSL." I didn't know what that meant, but the sales guy said it was the initials of Yves Saint-Laurent—you have to toss your head when you say it, *Yves Saint-Laurent*—a designer whose name even I recognized. I tried on the jacket and it… just…barely…buttoned. Hmmm. I'd never owned such a prestigious garment and I knew I was going to buy it. All I'd need to do was lose just a couple pounds more and the jacket would fit perfectly and I would be the sharpest-dressed guy in town and everyone would think I was cool. "Oh this old thing? It's Yves Saint-Laurent, of course."

Last year, I noticed something. That jacket was still hanging in my closet, after 26 years. I've never had it on. Never. It had become a visible reminder of how I've failed: failed to lose those extra pounds, failed to be the sharp-dressed fashion plate…failed to even clean out my closet every decade or so. That "YSL" might as well stand for "You

Stupid Loser" or "You're Still Large."

But if I've learned anything from that episode, it's this: Trying to fit into someone else's mold can be disheartening. People always say you should walk a mile in the other guy's shoes...but what if those shoes are way too big? Or worse, too small? Maybe I don't fit what you think of as the ideal man or husband. But I have a family who loves me and a God who thinks I'm pretty awesome. And I have learned that no matter how much weight I lose, there will never be room for anyone else in this skin except me. No matter how much I get lifted, lipoed, tucked, pierced, tattooed or electrolysized, I am still the same person.

So I tried instead to become comfortable with who I am. How comfortable? Comfortable enough to finally donate that navy blue blazer to Goodwill. And I didn't feel sad when I got rid of it; it was like getting rid of a nagging voice in my head. I'm hopeful that someday I'll see a guy at a stoplight, holding a sign and looking unusually dapper. And I'll stop and say, "Hey, lookin' good."

And he'll say, "Thanks...it's Yves St. Laurent."

Maybe I'm just not the designer clothing type...although I do frequently wear stuff by Yves Saint-Laurent's brother, Xavier Excalibur Laurent...that's why most of my clothes have his monogram inside: XXL. That's a designer whose clothes fit my lifestyle.

An empty hanger in my closet is all that remains of that jacket, except for this lingering thought--which applies to much more than clothes: if you spend your life trying to fit into someone else's outfit, you may never learn that you're destined for something...bigger.

I wrote that four years ago, when I was in Toastmasters. I did it at several humorous speech contests and won most of them. But there was something that didn't sit right with me, or—I now see—with the audiences who heard that speech.

It was the closing part, the part where I sort of justified being fat by implying that's really *just who I was.*

Not long after those contests, I started speaking professionally. I would stand in front of audiences and tell them that any problem, any challenge, in their lives could be solved by approaching it creatively.

And I realized I was not practicing what I preached. This weight thing that I had carried around my whole life was a very visible sign that I had not conquered all my challenges.

So I had to ask myself some tough questions. The biggest one was this: Was it possible to lose weight…creatively? How would that work?

I was stumped until I thought about my belief that we are each writing the story of our life every day. How would my story end? Well, the truth was that it would most likely end something like: "Mike dropped dead suddenly at age 62, due to complications brought on by obesity."

Uhhhh…I didn't like the sound of that at all. But how could I change the final chapter? I do not have the strongest willpower in the world. Cookies and potato chips are two of my four food groups as far as I'm concerned. How could I give them up?

When it comes to self-improvement, especially losing weight, people often say, "Do it for yourself."

Screw that. Virtually everything I've ever done has been for myself and where did that get me? It got me to 297 pounds. Yep, I was right there in the neighborhood of three hundred pounds and that was not a neighborhood I wanted to live in. I was fat because I did things "for myself." "For myself" didn't work as the reason I would lose weight.

See, I knew how to lose weight. I had that skill down. I'd done plenty of drill work on it, too, trying all those different diets. But what was the "thrill"? I couldn't lose weight for myself.

Cue the light bulb over my head.

I couldn't do it for myself. But I could do it for *you*. I could do it… for the story.

What if the last chapter of my life story—or one of the latter chapters, anyway—went more like this: "At the age of 59, Mike lost 75 pounds and got in the best condition of his life."

Which chapter would you prefer to read:

Mike drops dead of a heart attack?

Or:

Mike becomes a new person at the age most people stop trying to change?

As a writer and storyteller, the latter was much more enticing.

So I did it. In 2013, I lost 75 pounds.

How?

That's the wrong question. I told you before; *every* diet works for me.

The right question is Why?

And the answer is: it makes a better story…a more beautiful painting…a lovelier song.

I hasten to add that it was not as hard as you might think. Every day, I thought about the page of my life I was writing that day. Would it be a page about victory or one of defeat? When a pang of hunger would make my stomach growl, I chose to think about it as a literary device, a momentary setback or threat in the path of the story's hero. Just a little dramatic plot point. And when I put it in those terms, it was easier to decide to defeat the temptation and chalk it up as a victory.

After eleven months, I had lost more than just 75 pounds. My pants were eight inches smaller in the waist. I had got rid of all those XXL-size clothes; in fact, even the XLs were gone. I was no longer X-rated! I could see my toes again. I could tell what color underwear I had on without looking in the mirror.

I felt amazing, but not just because I was healthier. My confidence shot up. My thinking became more focused. I slept better, and snored less. I felt like I'd discovered my super powers.

There was one sobering truth I learned after I lost all that weight, though. A person who had heard me speak on several occasions congratulated me on taking off those pounds, but he also said something more truthful than he probably intended: "My wife and I always enjoyed hearing you, but we thought, 'Why can't he get control of *that* part of his life?'"

Maybe that seems like a rude comment to say to someone, but I was glad to get such an honest remark, because it made me conscious of something I had never considered before. Was it possible that the way I *looked* was speaking so loudly that it drowned out the things I *said*? This man unwittingly showed me that it was entirely feasible. That made my heart hurt a little, to find out that some people actually do judge a book by its cover. But it also gave me another sign that I had done the right thing by changing my appearance.

I wish that we didn't place such emphasis on physical attributes. Oh, you can prove your abilities—if you're ever given the chance—but it's like coming up to bat with one or two strikes already marked against you.

For years, I had told myself that it was okay to be fat. I was married, I wasn't trying to attract new admirers. I was a nice person. I was funny and smart and talented. Wasn't that enOugh?

I now realize that I didn't even see myself accurately in the mirror. I would stand in front of the medicine cabinet in the bathroom, looking at myself from straight on, and I could tell myself I looked okay. But then I would see a photo or video of me from the side and it would be a shock to see how big I was.

At the beginning of this chapter, I said I had a WEIGHT problem. I now know that what I had was actually a WAIT problem. I was waiting for something else to change me, for my dislike of exercise to somehow turn into a desire to run marathons.

I stayed fat...until—as Fats Domino sings—"I found my thrill..." That's when I was able to transform myself.

Regrets? Well, I'm sorry now that I gave that Yves St. Laurent jacket away. Although it would actually be too big for me now!

I was delighted to go buy new clothes, in sizes I hadn't seen since high school. I felt brand new and as though I could conquer the world.

But the best part was the story. As I write this, I'm 60 years old. Most of the people I know in my age group have started coasting. They believe that it's too late to change the way they are, so they'll just sit and wait.

I lost weight for them. I lost weight to prove to them that it is never too late to look for the Technicolor life.

You see, it's one thing to stand before people and tell them that you've found happiness or gotten wiser or learned to love. You can fake that. It's quite another when they can actually see the change. When I speak these days, I put up a picture of myself that I can hardly stand to look at. I'm about 295 pounds and wearing a shirt that looks like a tent. But when I stand right next to that picture—75 pounds lighter— that audience pays a lot more attention when I tell them the benefits of living creatively. They see the change. And then I tell them they can change, too.

So can you. If weight is your weak spot, please know that I've been there. You can tell yourself over and over that your life is fine just the way it is and besides, you have a slow metabolism, and you really don't eat that much.

You're living in black and white, dear reader. Don't you want to experience the Technicolor version?

You can always find an excuse for staying the way you are.

"It would be too hard."

"It would cost money."

"I'm too old."

"I don't know how."

Answer this question, then. How does your story end?

In November 2013, Joy Johnson became the oldest woman to finish the New York City Marathon at the age of 86, in spite of falling and hitting her head during the race. The next day, Joy Johnson died.

Most people think that's sad.

I think it's just about the best ending for Joy's story she could ever have hoped for. Just imagine: you set a record, you reach a pinnacle of success, you make it to the top of the mountain…and then you die. What a way to go! What a time to check out!

That's what I want to do. I have not yet reached my peak (see next chapter). Heck, I'm still not sure what I want to be when I grow up. But when I do reach that peak, I'm good to go. Take me out, coach. I'd much rather end on a high note than to die when my last notable achievement was twenty or thirty years earlier.

But while I'm still breathing, while my brain is still percolating, I'm going to keep looking for more…more skills, more drills, more thrills. 'Cause it's possible there might be something even beyond Technicolor.

I'll let you know.

# 13.

# WHAT HAVE YOU DONE FOR ME LATELY?

I've been planning to write this book for years, but it's probably a good thing I didn't get it done earlier.

Because I keep learning the Skill/Drill/Thrill lesson myself, over and over again.

There is a sad tendency among people around my age to stop believing. They don't believe in trying new things. They don't believe that people can change. And they certainly don't believe that they can still change themselves.

It's odd. I know people who won't watch a black-and-white movie because it seems old-fashioned and irrelevant, yet they don't know they're living a black-and-white life.

For me, life has never been more colorful.

I have one more story to tell you.

I gave my first speech in high school. I was at a district-level school competition in which there were all sorts of events. I was in a contest called Number Sense, which consisted of trying to answer 80 math questions in ten minutes. I finished the competition and was waiting around for my schoolmates to finish up with things like debate, poetry interpretation, and essay writing.

My English teacher told me I should try the Persuasive Speaking competition. I didn't even know what that meant, but she told me that you choose one of five topics or quesTions that you don't see in advance. You then have 30 minutes to prepare a seven-minute speech which should persuade listeners that your point of view is the best one.

I agreed to enter, though I had no preparation whatsoever. I entered a room with the contestants from other schools and saw that they had definitely come to compete. Some had rolling file cabinets, with folder full of clippings on every subject imaginable: the Vietnam war; hippies; drugs; pollution; politics…and other stuff I knew nothing about.

I picked my topic—can't remember now what it was—and set about trying to write a speech. The guy at the next desk was one of the Univac-brained kids with a filing cabinet and I asked if I could borrow a copy of Time magazine I saw in his stack of reference materials. He looked quizzically at me and then nodded his assent. I found a few statistics I could use and finished up my notes.

One at a time, we each entered the room where three judges sat. I stood behind the podium and began to speak, while wondering what in the world I was doing there. I talked. I gestured. And I put into practice the technique I learned from my preacher Daddy: when in doubt about your facts, pound on the lectern a little harder.

I pounded some lectern that day, my friends, and finished within the seven-minute time limit. Then I waited around for an hour until everyone had spoken and the judges had turned in their scored for tabulation and the results were posted on a bulletin board.

I won first place. I advanced to regional competition, won again, and eventually was in the state finals, where I won second place...only because I thought Vietnam was part of the Middle East. Oops.

I didn't do a great deal of speaking in the following years, although I often taught a teen Sunday School class; that was mostly just reading from the teachers book.

But when I began teaching my two adult classes, eight years ago, I was determined to do original content, not to buy curriculum from a bookstore. So I talked about things that interested me, things that were fresh on my mind. I had begun to listen to great storytellers, too, people like Garrison Keillor and Ira Glass and Bill Cosby. So my Sunday School lessons had some qualities not often found in churches: they were funny, they were entertaining, and they were interesting. After a few months, I had the idea to start using slides and video clips as part of my presentations. Unlike most dull PowerPoint shows, though, I had an extensive background in graphic design. Therefore, my slides were attractive and interesting on their own.

I also sought to expand my available subject matter. If we could learn a lesson from the story of Jonah and the whale, why couldn't we learn a lesson from the movie Groundhog Day? We could…and did.

That's when people began to say things like this: "We had a speaker at our annual convention last week who was terrible…really dull and stiff. I wish you could speak to our company."

Hmmm.

I helped start a Toastmasters group at our church and decided to go through the program. Although I thought I was already a fairly good speaker, I learned some things from Toastmasters, things like how often I said, "uhh" while speaking, and how to stand and move more naturally.

I started competing in Toastmasters contests and winning quite a few of them. Finally, I thought, I'm ready to start speaking profession-ally. I believed that all I had to do was announce that I was available and big money speaking gigs would start rolling in.

Not quite.

When I first thought of becoming a professional speaker, I had an image in mind. I could see myself—like Steve Jobs—onstage before a packed auditorium, standing in front of a massive projection screen while perfect lighting and sound enhance my every move, every word, and rapturous disciples waiting breathlessly for the next pearl of wisdom to fall from my lips.

That's what I pictured.

I did not picture this:

I stand in the back room of a Mexican restaurant in front of eleven people wearing club badges. Just as the president of the group introduces me, two waiters sweep in with the entrées and I am suddenly looking at the tops of eleven heads as they dig into their crunchy tacos and nachos and I begin my speech.

That's not how it was supposed to be. But that's how my speaking career began. After the fifth speech I gave in similar circumstances, I started to wonder about that vision which had once seemed so clear.

I had bought into the conventional wisdom that this was the path to speaker stardom: you spoke for free, anywhere you got the chance. You passed out business cards, tried to collect email addresses to build your list, and one of those attendees would eventually hire you for a paying gig.

It wasn't happening. I gave eighteen free speeches one year, and none of them led…anywhere. I spoke to the oldest Lions Club in the world, started ninety-nine years ago. I believe there were several charter members present when I visited. Some of them may even have been able to hear me.

What a waste of my time, right?

Wrong.

Those eighteen speeches were my baptism by fire, my paying of dues. If you can win over an audience whose main concern is the daily lunch special set before them, you've accomplished something. You've gained experience. You've tweaked your speech, taken out that line you always stumbled over, learned every possible connector that can go between a laptop and a projector. You've realized you'd better provide an intro to be read instead of letting Bobby Joe wing it.

And you've become a better speaker. Even if nobody knows your name yet.

19th century Scottish author Samuel Smiles wrote, "We learn wisdom from failure much more than from success. We often discover what will do, by finding out what will not do; and probably he who never made a mistake never made a discovery."

When you decide to make a big change in your life, you are probably going to fall on your face the first time or two. Maybe eighteen times! But you will eventually find the path that fits you.

I've never felt comfortable on the well-traveled path, the path "everyone else" is on. I've struggled to blog, to tweet, to coldcall, to shmooze. None of those ever seemed to fit me, but I was told that's how you have to do things.

Well, guess what? There are other paths to that vision, and if following someone else's footsteps feels too alien, trying cutting your own path through the jungle of the speaking business. Some of us will have to sneak in the back door or crawl through a window to make it to the main stage. So be it.

For me, those free speaking gigs were a way to work on my craft. It was definitely not glamorous, but it helped me grow. I changed out my entire opening. I learned how to make my slides something attractive and enhancing instead of a distraction. I found a path—my path. I eventually discovered my own voice, my tone, my sense of humor, my unique style. And I could not have done it without eleven people in the back room of a Mexican restaurant.

Keep plugging away. If you truly have something to say, you will eventually be heard. That vision you had may look a little blurry at the moment, like a mirage in the desert. But you're getting closer with Every. Little. Step

I joined the National Speakers Association and the local Austin chapter of NSA. I felt like such a novice at both places. I was surrounded by people who were making a living — a handsome living— speaking several dozen times a year. In the meantime, I was running out of available Rotary clubs and earning nothing but a free lunch.

I went to the NSA convention in Philadelphia. I only knew three people out of the 1500 who attended, and even those three I did not know well. I heard some great speakers and went to some helpful breakout sessions and got some good ideas, but my speaking career still seemed to be stuck in low gear. No, actually, it was stuck in "Park."

At age 59, was it ridiculous for me to try to start a new career? I loved speaking and truly believed I had a gift, but the business side of it was so foreign to me. Cold calls? Ugh.

I had forgotten my own formula, in spite of how many times it had worked for me. I had a definite skill and I had done considerable drill work on it. But I had not yet had the thrilling idea.

Hmmm.

At the Philly convention, I had been surprised to see that there was not a session devoted to improving the slides most speakers use in their presentations. I believed that I was doing some unusual things with my own slides, and I had hoped to pick up some new ideas.

A few months later, I reCeived an email from the National Speakers

Association, announcing a call for breakout presentations for next year's convention. Well, I thought to myself, I think I'll just apply to lead one of those sessions, one that'll be devoted to creating better slides.

I went to the online submission form and came up with a title for my presentation, told what the takeaways for attendees would be, and entered my biographical details.

The next page, though, asked for references, three NSA members who had seen me speak and could vouch for the value of my presentation.

Uh-oh.

I don't think a single professional speaker had ever heard me speak. Who could I list for references?

One man I'd met at the convention had been very helpful and friendly to me. I emailed him to ask if I could list his name, even though he'd never seen me perform. He had, at least, seen my website and looked at some video of me. He very kindly said he'd be glad to vouch for me. For the second reference, I entered the name of a lady who I had hired to give me some pointers on the speaking business. She was ninety years old, though, and also had not heard me speak in person. But I thought she might say nice things about me if asked.

Number three. I had no clue. I asked one speaker I knew slightly and she said no. I understood her decision; she had a firm policy of not recommending people she hadn't actually heard. I certainly saw her point, but it left me with a blank spot.

I couldn't come up with a third name, so I submitted the application with just two…two very tenuous connections at best.

Would it surprise you to learn that my application was declined? It didn't surprise me. It was a long shot, and it had not paid off.

A few days later, though, I received a group email from a woman who was putting together presenters for something called The Learning Lounge at the convention, a sort of alternate offering for those who couldn't find a breakout session that appealed to them. She encouraged all of us who'd been declined to think about combining with two or three others to form a block of programming for the Learning Lounge.

After some email conversations, I ended up in a group with three other speakers. Craig would be the facilitator and emcee. Christine would do sixteen minutes on crafting the introduction someone will read to introduce a speaker, how to write something that would set the speaker up to succeed with the audience. Judson would devote his sixteen minutes to sharing some interactive games to play with audiences to energize and engage them. And I would have sixteen minutes to tell professional speakers how to design slides that would not induce narcolepsy in their audience members.

Two months before the convention, the four of us had our one and only conference call to talk about how to structure our session. I had noticed that all of us were addressing aspects of being a speaker that didn't deal with the speaking part: intros, activities, slides. My original title for a breakout session about slides was going to be *No Power & No Point: Why Your Slides Suck & How To Make 'em Soar*. I saw no reason to change it, even though I was going to have a 16-minute slot instead of a 90-minute slot. I suggested that we call our group session *Taking The Suck Out Of Success*. The other three laughed and said that was fine.

That was the only time we spoke about the session, which would be held on the final morning of the convention in San Diego. Although this was my second year to attend, I was still feeling like a newbie. I had gotten to know the half-dozen Austin speakers who were there, but not many others. But I was still excited. I was actually going to be speaking at the National Speakers AssociatiOn convention.

Before the convention, I had thought about ways to publicize our session. It would be listed in the convention program, but it was competing with some big-name, hot-topic breakout sessions. The organizer had told us that if we had thirty or forty people in attendance, that would be considered a success. I was hoping to get more seats filled, so I turned again to my graphic design toolbox. I put together a nice flyer, full color, with pictures of us four speakers and brief synopses of our topics. I printed 200 copies of the flyer and took it with me, unsure of how I would distribute them.

The hotel was a huge place and I walked around looking for bulletin boards, but didn't find much. There were lounge areas where people would sit between sessions and then there was the grand ballroom where all 1500 of us would gather for general sessions, seated around banquet tables. I decided that would be my target. Each morning I would sneak into the ballroom while crews worked on lighting and sound, and I would place a couple of flyers on each table. I was waiting for someone to tap me on the shoulder and say, "That's not allowed in the ballroom," but no one ever did. I did the same thing before each general session. I also placed flyers on coffee tables in the lounge areas. When I met other speakers, I told them about our session, describing in glowing terms how great it was going to be.

For three days, I sowed my flyers like Johnny Appleseed.

Finally, the last morning dawned. I got to our assigned meeting room and made sure my laptop was hooked up and that the screen was bright and sharp and the lighting was not too harsh. I paced, waiting and hoping that thirty people would show up.

They began to trickle in and soon all our chairs were filled. We set up additional chairs and ended up filling most of them, too. By start time, 65 professional speakers were sitting in anticipation.

I did not meet Christine and Judson until just before we started. They were both very well known speakers, perhaps wondering why there was a no-name guy on the program with them.

Craig introduced the session and then Christine did her sixteen minutes, finishing to applause from the audience.

I was second. What was I doing there? I couldn't even find three people to say I was worthy of being on the program. But where slides were concerned, I had a definite skill and I had put many hours of drill work into making slides like nobody had ever seen.

I began quickly, trying to fit 90 minutes of material into sixteen minutes. The net effect of that was to make my segment jam-packed with usable content, not vague talk of goals and philosophies, but concrete examples and techniques these speakers could actually use. I am not exaggerating when I say that jaws dropped. During my sixteen minutes, I was interrupted four times by applause, simply because I had put something so unique and wonderful on the screen. When I finished my segment, I received a standing ovation from those professional speakers. I was exhilarated and a bit shaky.

Judson did his segment, received applause, and then we all returned to the stage for questions. Christine was seated next to me; she looked at me intently, then leaned over and said, "Where the hell have *you* been?"

I told her I was like Lana Turner, just sitting at the soda fountain, waiting to be discovered.

I was 60 years old and a brand new chapter of my life was starting off with a bang.

Several speakers who were in the audience that day posted on Facebook that my session was the highlight of the convention. People who had missed it were begging to know what I had shared. The hits on my website increased fifty-fold, from nine different countries.

In the next few weeks, I received many requests on LinkedIn, Facebook, Google+, and Twitter. So many people wanted to learn the tips I had shared that I decided to start a video podcast, incorporating and demonstrating the techniques I'd shown in San Diego as well as some new ideas. The video series, *ClickStarters*, very quickly had hundreds of views on YouTube and iTunes.

Two speakers who'd been in the audience contracted me to revamp their slides, compensating me very well for the job.

I decided to post an article I'd written on LinkedIn. Almost over-night I had more than 500 followers, with many more on the other social media outlets.

In the week following the convention, I booked three speaking gigs and had countless emails and messages from interested parties.

Oh, and guess what? Over a dozen well-known speakers offered themselves as references for next year's convention, all believing that I deserved a breakout session all to myself. I went from being a nobody to being the hot topic of conversation because of that sixteen-minute presentation. I might not have appeared to have the qualifications to speak to that group of people at that prestigious conference, but when the spotlight hit me, I was ready.

It works, my friends. Those three simple words keep changing my life, keeping it exciting, taking me to places I never thought I'd go. Even when I don't have a goal in mind, I've learned that sharpening my skills and doing the drill will help the thrill to show up eventually.

Mike Robertson

# 14.

# ODDS...& ENDS

I was finishing up this book a few days ago when an article appeared in a popular website. The writer of the piece stated that there was a real problem with the current crop of books, speakers and programs about creativity. The issue? Too many people using the same tired stories.

That's one of the major differences with this book, I believe. I have shared stories from my own life, stories that you have not already heard from multiple sources.

I don't do this for egotistical reasons, but merely because there is nothing more convincing than true personal experience. How do I know that thinking creatively can improve your life? IT HAS HAPPENED TO ME! AGAIN AND AGAIN!

The stories I've shared with you are by no means a complete list of creative outbursts in my life. Allow me to briefly mention a couple more before I wrap up.

Lisa and I built our first house in the country more than twenty years ago. We set about furnishing it and making it a home for us and our new baby. But for a long time we didn't get around to hanging pictures on the walls.

The walls in our house were all white and I grew tired of all that white space. We started painting some of the rooms in deep, rich colors and they looked much better. In the living room, though, I thought we could do something more. I wanted to paint a mural.

I hasten to add that I am not an artist with a paintbrush. But I am pretty handy with a computer. So I began putting together a picture on my computer, using bits of other images I found online, assembling an Art Deco-style cityscape of tall buildings and an ornate movie theatre. I added a zeppelin in the sky and a huge ship in the harbor. Two of the skyscrapers had our names on them.

Once I had the image on my computer, it was simple to print it out, draw a grid over it, and expand the grid to fill the wall space. I roughed out the shapes and we began to paint. Lindsey was three or four by then, and she even helped fill in some of the buildings.

When we were done, we had a completely unique centerpiece for our large living room. Cost? Only the paint. Value? Priceless. The deco cityscape was background for many great family photos and several fun parties. You don't create art because you're an artist; you become an artist because you create art.

Lisa was hired to do publicity for the church where I was already working. She had the job but no budget to do anything.

What's the first step, dear reader? Find the skill, the tool you already have. In this case, we had a new computer and a home video camera. We decided to produce a short newsreel to promote upcoming church events. It was produced in black-and-white with marching band music in the background and a deep-voiced narrator.

It was a hit with the church audience. Anything was an improvement over the "announcements" segment most church services have. From that first step, we grew more and more aMbitious. Each newsreel had a different style. We did a parody of *Monty Python & The Holy Grail*. We did a silent movie, complete with title cards and nickelodeon piano music. Lisa and I played characters from *Greater Tuna*. We did a home shopping channel newsreel and one that looked like a CNN broadcast. One newsreel was a black-and-white film noir detective story; through clever editing, we made our friends and coworkers interact with old Hollywood stars like Barbara Stanwyck and Edward G. Robinson.

By using the tools we had, and coming up with fun ideas, we did dozens of unique, creative presentations that always held the audience's attention while conveying the needed information.

And with that, my friend, we have reached the end. My fondest hope is that something in this book has sparked your imagination and that you are ready to do something wonderful.

I wish I had the power to tell you what you should do first. I can't. But I have given you the formula so that you can find your own path, tip-toeing through the pizzas, the peaches and the platypuses.

Take what you have, what you already know how to do.

Polish and sharpen that tool.

Go write a new chapter of your story that will surprise everyone.

Especially you.

# Enjoy Mike Robertson's other books:

# This Is Where I Came In

Mike's fascinating novel captures a period most people know nothing about: the birth of the motion picture industry.

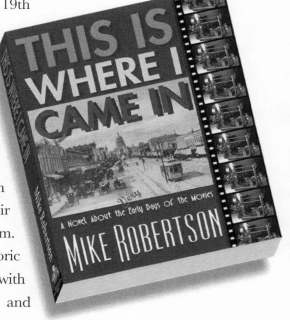

In the closing years of the 19th Century, young J.D. Wilkinson's small-town world is turned upside down when he witnesses the very first Texas exhibition of Edison's Vitascope machine. He becomes part of the first baby steps taken by the moving pictures in their move from novelty to art form. J.D. is present for some historic moments and crosses paths with people like D.W. Griffith and Buster Keaton in their formative years. *This Is Where I Came In* accurately portrays the pioneers whose adventurous spirits shaped the motion picture into the greatest media tool ever invented. Along the way, J.D. experiences the love of a mysterious woman and the hatred of a corrupt official. "I knew movies could capture life," J.D. says. "I just didn't know they would capture mine.

# Shiny Spots in the Rust

If you've read *The Pizza, the Peach & the Platypus*, you know that Mike Robertson can find stories just about anywhere. In *Shiny Spots in the Rust*, he shows that he can also find deeper meanings in many things that might seem trivial to most. This collection of brief, humorous-yet-inspirational essays is the sort of comfort book you can open at any page and get the boost you need for the day. Mike finds the humor and message in topics like flat tires, spelling bees, a bottle of Aqua Velva, and even dryer lint! Readers from age 12 to 92 have expressed their delight with this charming book.

*Man, is Mike Robertson funny. The average bulletin may not be a source of great literary wit and wisdom, but Robertson's writing in "Shiny Spots" is fresh and poignant and hilarious.*

—Eileen Flynn, *Austin American Statesman*

Does your business require you to do slide presentations? If so, you need to watch Mike Robertson's video podcast series, **ClickStarters**. In each free four-to-six-minute episode, Mike demonstrates tips, tricks and techniques to transform your slides from boring to amazing works of art.

# ClickStarters
## is available on
# YouTube
## and on
# iTunes

### Subscribe at either location to ensure you never miss an episode!

# About the Author

Mike Robertson is an award-winning speaker, author, musician and storyteller. With over a thousand hours of speaking experience, he has perfected a unique blend of humorous insight and motivation through personal stories with which everyone can identify. A lifelong Texan, Mike was winning state-level speaking competitions even in high school (which was longer ago than he'd like to admit).

A professional member of the National Speakers Association, his confidence, sense of humor and perceptive-though-quirky point of view make him what you always hope a speaker will be: memorable, entertaining and challenging.

Mike Robertson's historical novel, *This Is Where I Came In*, about the earliest days of the motion picture business, is part of the permanent collection at the Austin History Center. His second book is *Shiny Spots In The Rust*, a collection of brief humorous and inspirational essays. Fall 2014 will see the publication of his third book, *The Pizza, the Peach & the Platypus*, which is an accompaniment to his signature presentation on creativity.

Mike and his wife, Lisa, have been married for 27 years. They have one daughter, Lindsey, a University of Texas graduate, who is currently pursuing an acting career in New York City.

## Visit Mike's website: www.IsThisMikeOn.com

Mike Robertson

Made in the USA
San Bernardino, CA
28 August 2014